JJ THE AMERICAN STREET DOG

AND HOW HE CAME TO LIVE IN OUR HOUSE

written by

Diane Rose-Solomon

illustrated by

Rachel Cellinese

Acknowledgments

A very special thank you to Andy, Jamie and Zander Solomon for your support, love and invaluable input.

Huge thank you to Lisa Hacken for being my second pair of eyes.

Many thanks and much gratitude to:

Beca Lewis, Del Piper, Jet Tucker, Jamie Lewis, Barbara Budan, Michal McKeown, Kathy Piper, Corinne Pierce, Diana Cormier, Jan Ramsay, Lynn Medlin, Jennifer Fischman, Fran Lambert, Sam Bryant, Rob Bynder, Jennie Shafer Maguen, Barak Maguen, Megan Boyer, Leslie Berger, Kelly LaPlante, Laura Ripston, Kirsten Welles, Andrea Vecchione and Shoshanna Strauss.

Printed and bound in China on FSC® Certified paper with soy based inks.

Published by SOP3 Publishing
www.sop3publishing.com

Design by Jennae Petersen

ISBN 978-0-9857690-1-7
LCCN 2012915417

To JJ, who opened my eyes and heart to homeless and abused pets everywhere. May each and every one find the loving forever home they deserve.

ince as long as I can remember, I've wanted a dog.

At night, I dream about dogs. Little dogs with floppy ears and short legs. Big dogs with pointy ears and long legs. There are brown dogs, tan dogs and spotted all over dogs. Some are even pink and green.

But those dogs are just in my dreams.

We do have a cat named Kasey. I love Kasey. She stays in my room when I'm at school and comes out to greet me when I get home.

Dogs are different from cats. Not better or worse. Just different.

My parents have been telling me that having a dog is a big responsibility. "There's more to caring for a dog than just feeding him, Maya sweetheart. He'll need walks, and training, and checkups at the vet."

I promised to help feed and walk him, and I promised that I would love him with all my heart. They smiled and said, "We think we're finally ready too. In a few weeks we'll start looking for the perfect family dog."

I was so excited! I counted the days on my calendar until it was time.

A few nights later the phone rang. It was Uncle Jerry. My dad was listening to Uncle Jerry tell a story and every once in a while he would ask questions like: "How big is he? What does he look like?"

I tugged on Dad's shirt while he was talking, trying to find out what was going on.

It seemed like forever when FINALLY he said "OK, see you tomorrow," and hung up the phone.

He turned and said "hmmmph."

"What did he say?" I cried.

"Uncle Jerry was playing soccer, and when it was time to go home he was the last one there. It was getting dark out and he saw a puppy sniffing around the garbage. Uncle Jerry looked for tags on the collar but there were none. He also noticed that the choke collar was too tight."

"He brought him home to give him food, a warm place to sleep, and get that choke collar off. The problem is Uncle Jerry lives in an apartment building where dogs aren't allowed. Tomorrow he has to find a place for him to live."

"Can he come here? Pleeeease?" I asked.

Mom said, "I don't know if I trust a dog from the streets. What does he look like?"

Dad said, "Jerry says he has golden fur, floppy ears and a long snout. I'm going to meet him tomorrow."

Mom said, "OK, but we're just looking."

The next day I could hardly concentrate at school.
I just couldn't stop thinking about that dog.

That evening Dad pulled up in the car with the puppy. I skipped outside to greet them. That puppy was just about the cutest thing I had ever seen.

"Can we keep him?" I begged.

Even Mom had a big smile on her face. She said, "First of all, he's a dog from the streets so we should be careful." The puppy looked at her and wagged his tail so hard it looked like his backside was going to come off! His mouth was open and he seemed to be smiling.

I said, "Look, Mom, I think he's trying to tell us that he's just like every other dog."

"I agree that he looks sweet, Maya. But we also need to make sure he doesn't belong to someone."

That night, Uncle Jerry put signs around his neighborhood, placed an ad in the paper and contacted the local shelter to make sure no one was missing their dog.

Mom and I bathed the puppy while Dad went to the store to get him some good dog food, dog bowls, a few toys, a leash, a collar that fit and a cozy bed.

After he ate we all got to play. He loved to run, chew on his toys, play tug of war and chase tennis balls.

He also met Kasey, our cat. Kasey didn't seem to mind the puppy, though she didn't want to play, so she just slinked back into my room to go to sleep.

Then we heard a siren off in the distance. Dogs have supersonic hearing and the puppy heard it loud and clear. He stuck his snout right up in the air and howled! We all cracked up.

Finally Mom said I needed to get to bed and the puppy was probably getting tired too.

While Mom tucked me in I asked, "Shouldn't we give him a name?" Mom replied, "I suppose there's no harm in giving him a name at least for now."

We decided on "JJ" after my uncle Jerry who found him.

The next day, after school, we took JJ to the vet for a checkup. Dr. Welles said, "He looks like a healthy four-month-old puppy but he has fleas and worms, which is common for rescued animals."

Mom looked concerned.

Dr. Welles reassured her and said, "He probably lived with someone for a while, but it looks like he's been neglected. All he needs is a little tender loving care and he should be just fine." She gave him some medicine and a few shots to keep him healthy.

I asked Dr. Welles why the dog was out on a soccer field and not with a family.

She explained, "There are many homeless animals... some on the streets like JJ, and many others at shelters. There are wonderful organizations that rescue abused, neglected and homeless animals from the streets and shelters and place them in loving homes.

If you end up adopting JJ, that would be another dog rescued.

Plus, if you give him a simple operation called neutering, he won't be able to make more puppies, which is really important because right now there are more dogs than good homes for them."

Mom said, "Well, I had no idea. I thought we were just going to buy a dog. This changes everything. Of course we want to do the right thing."

Two weeks went by and no one had claimed him. Then one afternoon the phone rang. Mom answered it, and I could hear her saying, "Yes, the puppy is golden, of course you can come by." Mom hung up the phone.

My heart was in my stomach.

She said it was a nice lady whose dog got out when the gardener left the gate open. The lady noticed Uncle Jerry's sign and called us. The description she gave was very similar to our JJ.

I was terrified that she was going to take JJ away. I ran to my bedroom with JJ and sobbed.

Then the doorbell rang. I peeked out from my bedroom where JJ and I were hiding together. Mom answered the door.

Mom gently coaxed me out of the room with JJ. My face was puffy and my eyes were red from crying. I hugged the puppy tight. The lady took one look at him and said, "I'm so sorry to trouble you, but that's not my Muffin. My dog is smaller, is a girl dog and..."

Just then her cell phone rang. It was her neighbor calling to say she had found Muffin. Muffin was fine and would be safe until she got home. I've never been so relieved!

After the lady left, I looked up at my mom and quietly asked, "So, do you think we can keep him?"

Mom said, "It looks like JJ is our perfect dog now."

I jumped up and down so hard that I shook the house. JJ
saw how happy I was and he jumped up and licked my face.
My dream had come true.

We took lots of pictures of JJ, playing, running, snuggling with me on the sofa, and being loved. We even got one of JJ and Kasey napping together!

I brought my pictures in to school the next day so that I could tell all my friends about how Uncle Jerry rescued JJ and now he is our forever dog.

Author's note:

Our first dog, JJ, was actually found on a soccer field. When people would ask what kind of dog he was, I'd reply "An American Street Dog!" We didn't know what his mix was and he certainly wasn't a French Bull dog, or an Italian Greyhound, or a Welsh Corgi. It didn't really matter either. He was just JJ.

Not all pets are found on a soccer field like JJ. There are many animals living on the streets or in shelters and many of the shelters just don't have enough space. Adopting an animal from a shelter or rescue organization is one of the most important things you can do to help animal overpopulation.

For every animal that you adopt, you make room in the shelter for another in need. Additionally, it is estimated that a quarter of dogs living in shelters are purebred, if that is important to your family. Plus there are breed rescues for just about every breed. Moreover, most dogs purchased in pet stores are from puppy mills where many dogs suffer. Please be sure not to make an impulse purchase at the mall the next time you walk past a cute puppy in a window. That only perpetuates the problem. Reputable pet stores often invite rescue organizations for adoption days in their store.

Caring for a new pet is a big responsibility. Before you make that big commitment please be sure that you understand what it means for your family. Your new pet will need quality food, veterinary care, exercise, fresh water, a warm place to sleep and lots of love of course. Your pet will probably need obedience training, which takes some time, and patience. You'll need to have someone responsible care for your pet when you travel, and make arrangements for your dog to be cared for during the day if everyone works outside of the home. Don't forget to have your dog spayed or neutered to help decrease pet overpopulation.

Once you have established that you are ready to be a responsible pet owner, be sure to choose a pet with the right temperament for your family. All the love you give to your pet will come back to you many times over.

There are many resources for animal care and adoption available. Please visit my website Save Our Pets People and Planet (www.sop3.com) for more information.

A percentage of the proceeds of this book will be donated to appropriate animal rescue organizations.

Please look for more books in the "JJ" series coming soon! (sop3publishing.com)

© 2012 Diane Rose-Solomon

About the author

Diane Rose-Solomon, a Certified Humane Education Specialist, rescued the real JJ 17 years ago. This is her first book, and the first in the "JJ The American Street Dog" series, with four more in the works. Ms. Rose-Solomon lives in Los Angeles with her husband, two children and two rescued dogs, Gonzo and Ninja.

About the illustrator

Rachel Cellinese is a graphic designer and illustrator living in Los Angeles. She also uses her artistic talents to help organizations such as 826LA and Big Class New Orleans. This is her first full-length children's book. One day she hopes to adopt a dog of her own!